Your Daily Homemade Bread Easy Stand Mixer Bread Recipes

Your Daily Homemade Bread

Easy Stand Mixer Bread Recipes: *Best Basics*

Mary Ellen Ward

www.thehomemadehomestead.com

May 2014
First Print Edition

All Rights Reserved
ISBN: 1499634722
ISBN-13: 978-1499634723

Dedication

There is really only one person I could dedicate my first bread book to: the original bread-hound himself; the boy, almost man, after my own heart choosing a warm slice of soft white bread over any sweet treat; the one who is always coming back for just one more piece: my son, Timothy.

Table of Contents

Who DOESN'T Want Homemade Bread Every Day?

If you could, you would eat homemade bread every day. Who wouldn't? It's healthier; it's cheaper; it's fresher; and it's just plain better. When you bake your own bread you get to control everything that goes into this primary staple; you have the comfort of knowing exactly what each ingredient in it is and how your bread was handled every step of the way.

Everyone has fond memories of both the taste and the smells of homemade bread. So why *don't* we just go homemade?

The reasons are obvious. Making traditional homemade bread is time consuming. It's a laborious, messy process that we just plain don't have enough time in our busy modern lives for...maybe once in a while as a treat, as a nice addition to dinner, but as an everyday staple, an everyday diet item, no one has the time to keep up with real homemade bread.

Unless, of course, you have a stand mixer, as many of us do (we'll assume you do if you've purchased this book – if not, it's HIGHLY recommended you buy one – it's a purchase you WILL NOT regret!). KitchenAid® might be the most famous of the stand mixers, but basically any good stand mixer is equipped to do the job of mixing and kneading your bread in very short time, making it possible for *you* to make homemade bread a menu item each and every day.

The trick to being able to regularly and reliably make your own homemade bread lies in a few things:

- having the right tools for the job (namely, a good stand mixer)
- having a simplified process that takes the major work out of bread-making to make it manageable
- having reliable recipes you like, that fit the requirements above

Buying the mixer is the easy part. It's the recipe and process simplification that can pose the challenge. That's where this book comes in.

A Bit About Myself & My Household's Diet

Very quickly, allow me to tell you a bit about myself and how this recipe collection came to be. I am a homesteader and writer, head poultry-raiser, wife, and mother of four. Over time we have become quite committed to eating better—more wholesome, more *known* foods—in my household. We eat a more traditional diet with real fats and raise almost all of the meat and vegetables we eat; we keep a couple of friendly cows in the backyard that provide for all of our dairy needs and we cook and bake most our foods from scratch. Including all of our breads. Now if you caught that, that makes us a family of six. All of my kids are currently school-age. And that makes for a lot of bread to get us through.

The only way to maintain our food standard is for me to find *manageable* ways to do so. I personally define "manageable" as something I am able to fit into my ever-evolving, busy, frequently disrupted daily schedule. And as much as I loved Grandma's hand-made, homemade bread, her version just isn't going to fit my life in these modern times; not, at least, for everyday eating. (Add to that the fact that I have a personal aversion to hand-kneading and floured-surface messes, and we're really in a bit of a bind here.) I take nothing, of course, away from Grandma; few women could hold a candle to her, myself included. But just as she did, we all have to find the ways that work for us and still prioritize what's best for our own.

How do we do that?

We use the tools we've been given and we simplify the process down to something that fits without sacrificing the elements that are really important to us. What matters most to me is that I am able to provide my family and visitors with good, hearty, wholesome food that is not laden with a laundry list of unnecessary ingredients and chemical preservatives. We need to like it. It needs to be affordable. It needs to be good.

Tools of the Trade for the Modern Home Bread-Maker

As tools of the manageable home bread-making trade go there are basically two. The first that probably comes to mind is a bread machine. They have their place and I actually relied solely on one for several years. But they have their limits, too, and I think we all agree that while their resulting product is good, convenient, and still better than store-bought, there's something about it that's not quite right. When I was still using my bread machine I ended up just using the dough cycle anyway and then baking the breads and doughs in my oven. So when it broke, it made sense to turn to my KitchenAid® instead (the stand mixer of course being the second of the two tools).

As it turned out this was an even better solution. Not only was the resulting bread better, but I was able to always make a two-loaf batch at a time, something the bread machine could never do. I always *needed* two loaves, but had to do sequential batches to get them. So in effect the KitchenAid® ended up saving me time overall along with giving me better bread.

Simplifying the Home Bread-Making Process

That answers the question of the right tools, so the only issue left is simplifying the process. Some people simply use their stand mixer and run through a typical, traditional bread recipe and process, just using the dough hook instead of your hands. There's nothing wrong with that but it doesn't really fit my criteria for daily manageability. The traditional bread-making process is somewhat long and drawn out and includes multiple steps and multiple waiting periods. I really need something that fits into a (relatively) few snatched minutes or something I can do as I'm attending to other kitchen or cooking matters. The general process used for the KitchenAid® breads in this book fits this order and still gives me an excellent product (you'll learn more about the process in a later section).

It is for this reason that you will find there is actually a lot of similarity between recipes in this book, at least as far as the preparation and processing goes. For a number of recipes the only real difference is in the ingredient list. That makes a lot of sense because basically the process of making bread is pretty predictable; but you will find the process a little bit different from what you are used to if you are more of a traditional, hands-on bread baker. If you're not, you'll likely just find it a good new way to make bread.

The up side to this is that once you are familiar with the process you'll find it easy to switch things up and try new recipes in this book. As a matter of fact you'll more than likely settle on a couple of your own fan-favorites and know them by heart quickly enough, not even needing the recipe for your favorite stand-by's. Still, it is worth noting that you can expect a lot of process similarity, and that simple changes to ingredient lists are often all that's needed to create a new, delicious, bread for your pantry or table. You'll learn more about the options when we talk about substitutions and that is sure to give you some good ideas for some minor changes that give big results.

I'd definitely recommend that you play around with ingredients to come up with flavors and creations all your own (and I'd certainly love to hear of your results!). What do you have to lose but a few minutes of time and a few cups of flour? But whether you decide to experiment or go "by the book," you're sure to find that the recipes in this book do just what they're intended to do – provide you with excellent options for homemade bread that you can make easily at home to help you put better foods on your table.

Getting Familiar With Your Stand Mixer As Bread Maker

The KitchenAid® Mixer and its many peers are excellent machines capable of performing many duties. With the right fittings and attachments your mixer can be anything from a meat grinder to a ravioli maker. Many of us don't know the half of what our stand mixers can do, or the most appropriate ways to make them do it (and again, I include myself in this category! It seems my KitchenAid® always has something new to teach me). In the interest of getting the best results in bread- and dough-making, and in the interest of protecting the longevity of your machine, it's worth a quick discussion on what the right attachments are to use when making heavy bread doughs.

There are really just a couple of attachments you want to familiarize yourself with for this particular use, and they are all things that come standard with the majority of stand mixers.

The Bowl

Of course you need your vessel, your mixer bowl. The only thing to really know about your stand mixer bowl is that you want it to be able to fit the ingredients for these recipes, which are larger than typical cake and cookie recipes. Most recipes will make two loaves of bread at a time and for that you'll be using about 6 ½ to 7 cups of flour as a base, plus additional ingredients. The average bowl that comes with a stand mixer is 4 ½ (+) quarts and is equipped for the job. If yours is smaller than this, I'd suggest taking a minute to see how much it can hold (at least measure in 7 cups of flour and make sure it can easily hold that).

Mixing Attachments

What is more important to know is which mixing attachments are the right attachments to use. Using the KitchenAid® as our example (due to its popularity and recognizability), choose the closest attachment for your stand mixer or your specific KitchenAid® model to perform each task.

You will use two different mixing attachments when you make bread and dough using the recipes in this book. The first attachment you will use will be for the mixing of ingredients and bringing the dough together. For this step I recommend using the flat beater (sometimes called the "paddle" attachment). If you do not have a flat beater with your stand mixer, the dough hook would be a better choice than a wire whip.

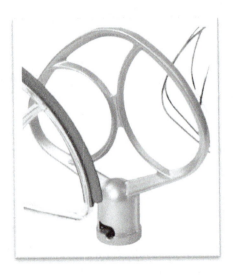

FLAT "PADDLE" ATTACHMENT FOR KITCHENAID® MIXERS
(Attachments vary in shape by model, but will look similar to this; use the closest attachment for your stand mixer.)

The flat beater is much sturdier than the wire whip beater and will stand up to the job of mixing heavy doughs time after time. The wire whip will not. It will do the job, but it's likely to come out of shape once the heavy dough pulls together. It is also very difficult to get the mixed dough out of the wire beater. With the flat beater (or paddle as some like to call it), a few taps is all it takes to remove the bread dough from the beater.

The second attachment you will be using is the dough hook.

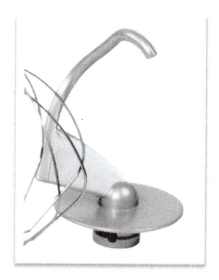

DOUGH HOOK ATTACHMENT FOR KITCHENAID® MIXER
(Again, exact size and shape will vary by model; use the closest attachment
for your specific mixer.)

This sturdy piece is expressly designed for the task of kneading bread doughs and the like, and it does an excellent job of it. You'll only use the flat beater long enough to mix and pull the dough together. Once it forms a ball you'll switch over to the dough hook and let the hook take all the work out of kneading for you.

If you have a splash guard (depending on your model) you may or may not find that helpful as well but it's not a critical feature, just a sometimes-mess-saver.

That is truly all you really need to know about your mixer and its varied attachments in order to make bread with your stand mixer. As mentioned there are numerous other things that your KitchenAid® and like rivals can do, and those things are fun to explore, too, but for today this is enough. Not so hard, now, is it?

The Basic Method for Basic Stand Mixer Breads

The same basic method is used for all of the recipes in this book because it is the fastest and easiest way to make good homemade bread and it reliably delivers an excellent product. In addition, using one basic method for a variety of recipes makes the life of the baker easier – once you make a few breads and have the basic steps down, you'll find it easier and easier to prepare fantastic breads in short time. In fact, you're very likely to memorize your favorite recipe completely!

In simplified terms, the steps of this basic method are as follows:

- combine together all dry ingredients and the fat (butter, lard, oil, etc.), *including* the yeast
- use very warm liquids and pour into the dry ingredient/fat mixture, then mix through (around 120°- 130°F – your hottest tap water in most homes, this being the range recommended for home hot water heaters)
- use the dough hook attachment to knead the bread for about 7 minutes
- let the dough rest for a short period, as per recipe (usually 10 minutes)
- shape the dough into loaves and rise until doubled, then bake

If you are familiar with traditional methods of baking bread, you probably picked up on a few usual steps in the process that are missing. (If you're not familiar with traditional bread-baking, don't worry; you'll have no trouble catching on to this easy stand mixer method!) Those steps include "proofing" the yeast in a luke-warm liquid and an added long first-rise period, followed by punching down, shaping, and more rising. These are the steps that make baking homemade bread a long and involved process. Not necessarily a tedious process (it can be quite enjoyable to make slow foods when time permits), but definitely a process that few people have the time for on a regular basis in today's very busy world.

The absence of these steps is not a mistake; nor is adding the yeast in with the dry ingredients. When you use this basic stand mixer bread method, you don't *need* these extra steps and time. The key is really all in the yeast that is used and its own unique action (more on that in the next section).

What then, is the result? How does this bread compare to other, more traditional baking methods?

To answer that question, let's first say this: any baking method and any recipe is going to result in something a little bit different. That is, after all, why we *have* so many different methods and recipes—to serve a different purpose; to create something new; or to ease a process.

That said, you are absolutely sure to be pleased with the results of this faster, easier, basic bread method. The results are comparable to traditional bread baking results, and many people find them to be superior even to recipes they have prepared the traditional way. A lot depends on your personal skill and ability. Some of us struggle with hand kneading and getting it "just right". A lot depends on how well-suited your home and even your location is to rising and baking bread. Homes where rising has proven difficult often get a better result from this bread that requires less rising and utilizes a more active yeast to begin with. A lot depends on the time and effort you have available to you for preparing your bread supply—the proverbial "hours in a day". It may be the case that you have a really stellar traditional bread recipe, but hardly ever any time to prep and bake it, and so maybe a "nearly" stellar recipe that you can make in minutes on a regular basis really proves to be the better choice.

Even putting all of that aside, this bread method in and of itself has proven to be reliable time and time again, capable of delivering a highly desirable product. When you factor in the fact that your bread is fresh and includes only minimal, reasonable ingredients, ingredients you know, approve, and recognize, and the fact that with this manageable method you can eliminate hidden chemicals and preservatives from your bread, it's a winning proposition all around. In the end you have a fast bread method that requires only about 15 minutes of active preparation time (the rest of the time is really just rising and baking while you go on to other pressing things) comparable to quality bakery breads for a fraction of the cost. That makes it very hard to lose.

Troubleshooting the Basic Bread Method

You now know the basic steps to baking bread with this method. It really is a pretty straight-forward and forgiving method; nevertheless bread sometimes can have a mind of its own, it seems, and so it helps to look at some simple tweaks and troubleshooting methods that might make the process that much easier for you.

In many ways making bread can be very "personal" in that the specific factors in your home will differ from those of another, possibly even from your next-door neighbor's, and so it helps to familiarize yourself with a few of the tricks of the trade that can make the difference. Please note that NONE of this is said to deter you from trying to bake your own bread. Quite the opposite! This is only said to give you a leg-up and help you overcome some potentially small hurdles that can make a big difference in the breads you bake.

When things go wrong with baking bread, it is almost always an issue with the bread not rising well. After that the issues usually have to do with things like structure or falling after rising. If you find the results of a bread batch to be not quite to your liking, there are a few things you can try to do differently:

- First, before doctoring a recipe too much, try the recipe again. It's surprising what a difference a day can make with bread, and often nothing different needs to be done at all. As you bake bread more often you'll come to learn the little things that can negatively impact the outcome and you'll learn to adjust for different circumstances of the day (for example, dry air or cool temperatures). Know that we all have our good days and bad days and in the end you're out a bit of time and a few ingredients – nothing that should make you give up! If that doesn't work, try some of these other suggestions:

- Increase the yeast (keep it to a minimum and take care – too fast a yeast action can cause a weak gluten development and structure, and result in falling breads. For these recipes probably no more than ¼ to ½ teaspoon extra).

- Purchase new yeast. Yeast is alive and old or improperly stored yeast can become highly inactive and even die and stop acting completely. If it's been a while or your yeast was exposed to warm temperatures or humidity, buy new. Store yeast in a cool, dry place, or better yet, in your freezer.

- Change yeast brands. It's just a fact that some yeasts perform better than others and some brands will prove to be more reliable for you. If one yeast doesn't seem to be doing the trick, try a completely different brand. (Although I've successfully used a number of different brands, my favorite is Fleischmann's Instant Yeast for these recipes – more on that coming up.)

- Knead more. A dry, coarse bread can result from not kneading the dough long enough, which does not allow the gluten to develop. In theory over-kneading can also cause texture and structural issues, but it's generally accepted that, practically speaking, neither you nor your machine could or would over-knead a bread dough. That's not to say you should go crazy with the kneading, but if you need to adjust your kneading time, go to the longer end of the range given (and possibly a minute or two longer).

- Find a better place to let your bread rise. The area where you place your bread to rise should be warm and as draft-free as possible. Cool temperatures retard yeast growth, and too cool a spot or a spot that is open to cool or cold drafts will do the same.

- Be aware of humidity when rising. This is especially an issue in dry winter months or in very dry climates. Yeast likes moisture as well as warmth. When the air is too dry, rising can be difficult. Let a pan of water simmer on a stove burner to humidify the room or consider rising your dough in a warmed oven with a pan of boiled, steaming water on the bottom shelf. (Only warm the oven on its lowest setting and shut the oven OFF before putting the dough in to rise. Do not cover the dough when you rise in the oven – the humidity of the enclosed space will be plenty and can cause a sticky top if covered, which can stick to the cover and cause your nicely-risen loaf to fall. Remove the water pan prior to baking.)

- Sift or spoon your flour when measuring. The major ingredient in your bread dough in terms of bulk is your flour. If you are not sifting your flour or are not spooning it into the cup when measuring, it's easy to get a dense measurement and therefore too much flour. (Let me admit here, however, that I hardly ever take that much care with measuring the flour in these recipes using this method. The whole point for me is good bread in record time, and these recipes usually forgive my haste. Please don't tell Grandma!). Still, it's worth mentioning and worth a try if you're having troubles. You might even find it's more of an issue with some flour brands as opposed to others.

- Let your cold ingredients warm up before mixing. This is really a flour issue since it is by far the largest volume ingredient in your bread. A tablespoon or three of cold sugar won't impact the outcome much, but six *cups* of flour is a different story. If your flour is stored refrigerated or in a cold pantry or cabinet, let it sit in a warmer room for a little while and warm to room temperature before mixing. It can have a big impact on the activity of the yeast.

- Raise your rising patience level. We all know we can't control the weather, and sometimes honest-to-goodness weather factors are in more control of your bread dough than you are. We know temperature and humidity have a significant impact, but so, too, can things like atmospheric pressure and storm systems. You won't be able to fight these factors so control what you can and accept that sometimes you might just need to give it a little more time to rise. Typically with this method 1 to 1 ½ hours will be sufficient (and some recipes, like the French Bread, may rise even quicker than that), but know that rising time is subject to many factors and is variable. Don't give up on your bread for a lack of patience! Give it some time.

- Decrease rising time. Many things with bread seem paradoxical and just as rising for too short a period can cause issues, so too can letting your dough rise for too long. Over-risen bread will become too gassy and yeasty, affecting both the flavor and the structure. Over-risen bread will stick to the cover, collapse when it is removed, and/or fall by itself and leave you with a dense, flat bread when baked. It's a simple fix, but do be aware that in the warmer months and in humid weather you'll want to keep a closer eye than usual as your bread under these conditions can rise much faster than expected or faster than what is written in a given recipe.

- Adjust your expectations and be aware of different rises for different flours. Sometimes what you think is a failure really is not. Refined white flours just make lighter loaves and rise higher than whole grains. In fact, whereas you should rise your white breads to double their initial size, with whole grains you will normally only expect to get somewhere between 1 ½ to 2 times the size. This is not a mistake; it's just the way of working with whole grains. Relax, experiment, and get to know the recipes you love best.

- Listen to your mother (grandmother, grandfather, baking friend, whomever). This list of troubleshooting tips is by no means exhaustive. You can learn a lot from people with experience, so always keep an open ear and mind for more helpful tips!

- Keep on baking! When it comes down to it, who cares if a loaf or two goes awry? We all have "those days" and the best way to overcome them is to just try again. You'll find this method and these recipes to be pretty forgiving and well-performing, but there is actual science to becoming more successful by baking bread more often – a kitchen where bread is baked more regularly becomes more conducive to successful bread baking. The more bread you bake, the more wild yeasts that will be in your kitchen, and those will only help make your environment friendlier to bread baking as you go along. Good news!

The Fast Talk on Fast-Acting Yeasts

The method in this book works because of the type of yeast that is used. It's a type that home bakers are less familiar with, is relatively new on the yeast scene, and not everyone can even find readily under its given name (which does NOT mean it's not there for you – read on). Because of this, familiarizing yourself with the usual yeast options is a few minutes well spent.

There are really only three kinds of yeast that most modern home bread makers encounter in recipes. In fact, most people probably aren't all that familiar with the third, which is actually the yeast all of these recipes use and is the yeast that makes this fast method possible. (*Fresh or Cake yeast is excluded in this discussion as it is limited in availability and not a typical yeast home bread makers use.*)

The first yeast home bakers usually know is Active Dry Yeast. This is your regular, regular acting, traditional dry granulated yeast that is most commonly packaged in paper-foil envelopes and is widely available in grocery stores. Active Dry is what is called for in most traditional home bread recipes. It is dormant and needs to be proofed in a warm liquid before it can be used successfully in a bread recipe. In addition to proofing before you start it requires two separate rises and periods of rest.

The second type commonly known is Bread Machine Yeast. Bread machine yeast works in bread machines because it is made up of smaller, more active yeast granules. These granules absorb liquids more quickly and so they do not require proofing in liquid to activate them. Instead, they are added directly to the dry ingredients and perform very well. Bread Machine Yeast often (depending on the brand) has an added dough conditioner, ascorbic acid.

The third type of yeast, the one used in this book, is Instant Yeast. Instant Yeast is essentially the same thing as Bread Machine Yeast; in fact, for some brands, it is *exactly* the same thing. Instant yeast is just what we discussed above under Bread Machine Yeast: a smaller-granule yeast that combines directly with dry ingredients, is fast-acting, and saves steps since it does not require proofing. Instant Yeast does not need two rises to make good bread. It requires only one short (usually ten minute) rest period between kneading and final shaping and rising. It is these characteristics that make the basic stand mixer bread method possible and successful, and that give you the ability to produce excellent fresh breads any day of the week with very little hands-on work.

In essence it is fair to say that Bread Machine Yeast and Instant Yeast is the same thing. It can, however, be a little more difficult to find Instant Yeast labelled as such in a typical grocery store. Some companies use exactly the same product, just labelling it differently to suit the recipe requirements of different customers. Fleischmann's Yeast, for example, sells the same exact product three different ways: as Instant Yeast, Bread Machine Yeast, and Rapid-Rise™ Yeast (Rapid Rise is simply a trademarked product name and is no different from the other two, but is often easier to find than Instant or even Bread Machine in a limited market). Many other companies do this as well but for all intents and purposes all you really need to know is that Instant Yeast, Bread Machine Yeast, or a rapid-type yeast will all work for you in these recipes and you can use whatever is most convenient and most readily available to you.

As with any baking product, you might find that a given brand of yeast works better for you than another. If you find your breads are not performing as desired, trying a new brand of yeast is advisable. To help keep costs down and to make it easier to have enough yeast on hand for all the bread baking you will be doing, the best way to buy your yeast is usually by the jar or by the vacuum-packed "brick". Wholesale clubs often sell bricks of instant yeast at a low price and ordering it online is also a very affordable way to stock up. Store yeast in a cool, dry place and after opening consider storing it in the refrigerator or freezer (especially during the summer) to maintain its activeness and freshness. If your yeast is past its expiration date, gets moist, or seems to act slowly, you should replace it.

Longevity and Life Factors for Stand Mixer Breads

One thing people typically want to know when baking their own breads is, *How long will it last?*

We all know that the plastic-packaged breads on a store shelf are far from freshly made by the time they reach their point of purchase, including many bakery and "homemade" versions. The way these breads are kept soft, palatable, and fresh is to add things like preservatives and dough conditioners. The entire point (or a very large factor in it, at least) of making your own homemade bread is to avoid these extra, questionable chemicals. And so, we simply cannot expect that we will get the same shelf life out of a cleaner, simpler, homemade bread.

Ideally, the perfect time to eat most homemade breads is about a half an hour after they've come out of the oven while still warm enough to melt a pat of creamy butter. But that's just spoiling ourselves (but do go ahead— indulge!!). Understanding this and all those factors previously discussed, the breads in this book will hold up quite well over a course of days. Under good storage conditions (cool, dry, preferably not refrigerated), these breads will still impress after two or three days with little noticeable difference. When not challenged by environmental conditions (like high humidity and high temperatures), these breads will be clean and consumable for as long as a week (with some loss of moisture and texture, as is to be expected).

As we see with store-bought breads, the shelf life of your breads will be determined by those environmental factors mentioned here and that also means that the life and longevity of your breads might even be different at different times of year (for many of us with changing seasons, it certainly will be). Either way, even under the worst storage conditions you can generally expect your bread to last well for at least two days. Fortunately these recipes are easy enough to prepare while you are in the kitchen making dinner or attending to other matters, and so even during the times of year when storage might be more of a challenge for you, mixing and kneading a couple of good, fresh loaves will be easy enough for you to do as needed. After all, that's the point – to be able to have excellent, healthy bread virtually on-demand.

A Quick Note On Fats and Substitutions

Depending on your dietary preferences, demands, and beliefs, you may prefer to change the fat (lard, shortening, oil, or butter...) in a given recipe to better suit you. Generally speaking, this is easily done in any of these recipes, with little impact on the outcome.

You'll find the recipes in this book use fairly basic fat sources and often very traditional ones like lard and butter. The fats used herein have been chosen over manipulated and hydrogenated ingredients (such as store-bought lard, which is hydrogenated, and shortenings—when lard is called for in a recipe in this book, real, rendered, non-hydrogenated lard is preferred), and mainly for matters of personal preference. It happens to be my personal belief (supported by a number of sources and emerging research), that more real, natural, unadulterated fat sources are more digestible and manageable for our bodies, possibly indicated in cancer and free-radical prevention, and also sources of fat-soluble vitamins and vitamin accessibility, and so that is what I choose to use. Note this is not an attempt to preach one dietary or nutritional belief over another, simply to explain the sources and options.

That said, there is no reason that a vegetable shortening or store-bought, shelf-stabilized lard cannot or should not be used if that is what you prefer. You should choose whatever ingredient is most affordable and preferable to you and our family. Generally speaking (and you should try the recipe your way once or twice to find out for yourself), you can easily substitute one fat for another; for example, shortening for lard or vice-versa, butter for either one, oil for butter, butter for oil, or butter and lard interchanged. Simply use the same measurement of the fat you prefer in exchange for what is called for in the recipe. (Note that butter should always be softened at least to room temperature for mixing purposes.)

You may also choose to make changes and substitutions to flours and sweeteners as well. You might like to substitute a whole-grain flour for some or all of a white flour; you might substitute a whole-grain white flour for all-purpose; you might use bread flour in place of all-purpose. All of these are totally acceptable substitutions. Just realize that different flours, particularly whole grain wheat, etc., act differently than white flours and so your results will differ accordingly (this is why an attempt was made to deliver a range of basic, everyday breads that already provides you with different dietary options and flavors).

On the subject of flour substitutions, you will note that the recipes in this book do call for all-purpose white flour over bread flour or over whole-grain white flour. While this is intentionally done, by no means does it mean that you should not use a whole-grain white flour or bread flour. The only reason that all-purpose was chosen is to keep these recipes as affordable and simple as possible, and to take advantage of the ingredients people are more likely to have in their stock of baking staples. In fact, bread flour is likely to deliver an even better rise and texture, but all-purpose performs very well without the added expense and trips to the store. If you make a regular practice of baking most or all of your own bread, you'll come to appreciate the cost savings.

One final note on the subject of flours – vital wheat gluten, a natural protein ingredient available for purchase in the baking aisle, may be added to all-purpose flour and/or recipes containing whole-grain wheat and other whole-grains. Vital wheat gluten is, essentially, what makes the difference between all-purpose flour and white bread flour. When added, it will improve the texture and rising of breads made with these flours. If you have difficulty with rising and texture, or if you would like to improve a little on the texture of a given recipe, try adding 2 to 3 tablespoons to your dry ingredients (less if you feel the result is too soft or spongy). This can also be a particular help to people living and baking at high altitudes, where rising is often more difficult.

Sugar and other sweeteners perform an important role in bread-making, and more than just taste. Sugars are essentially "food" for the yeast. Without added sweeteners, there is only a limited amount of natural sweetener in the flour available to the yeast for it to act on. This will result in a low- and slow-rising dough and a chewy product; this is ideal for making things like pizza dough, but not a good characteristic for bread. For this reason, it is not recommended that you substitute an artificial sweetener for other sweeteners in yeast bread recipes.

What is possible is to slightly decrease the amount of sugar in a recipe (by about 1/3), or to exchange the sweetener called for in the recipe for another type of natural sweetener. Brown sugar, white sugar, molasses, honey, maple sugar, maple syrup, and corn syrup (light or dark) can all be used interchangeably in bread recipes for the most part. Substitute in at the same measurement called for, but do be aware that if you are substituting a liquid sweetener (honey, molasses, etc.) for a granulated or dry sugar you may need to decrease the liquid in the recipe, and/or you may find it necessary to add additional flour in the end. This can result in a slightly different texture and rising, so it's something you'll want to experiment with.

You should also note that different sweeteners (honey and molasses in particular) will cause more darkening of the crust (and/or *faster* browning as well), so when exchanging a sweetener you will want to keep an eye for doneness. Decreasing the oven temperature by 25° or tenting the bread with foil for the final ten minutes can help eliminate over-browning.

Of course, changing the sweetener can also impart a different flavor – sometimes minimal and sometimes a great difference – but the outcome can be very good, too. In the end, experimenting with sweetener substitutions can deliver a new, delicious product without having to learn an entirely new recipe. At any rate *most* substitutions do not result in a poor product, just a different one and it's worth a try at least once if you're curious or working to achieve something specifically to suit your diet.

Make-Ahead Options

The method and recipes in this book have been selected for their convenience and because they make it more possible to bake fresh bread in short time on a regular basis. The idea is that with a quicker and easier method, you can make bread virtually whenever you need to. However, life in the modern world is a busy thing and sometimes even fast work is just not enough to fit into it.

If more convenient, you can prep your bread doughs ahead of time (such as on a free afternoon, a weekend, etc.) and freeze for later use. To do this, prepare the recipe as normal and let the dough go through its ten-minute rest period. You can then shape the dough into a loaf and freeze it. When you are ready to bake your dough, place the frozen shaped loaf into a greased bread pan, cover, and leave in a warm place (or moist warm oven, shut off) to thaw and rise. (Some people prefer to shape the dough into a flattened disk which will store more easily and thaw more quickly, but requires more handling on the other end. If you do this, thaw the disk, roll into loaf shape, then rise in the pan as normal.)

Making dinner rolls ahead can be particularly helpful as you can make large batches of dough and then shape the individual rolls, freeze, and bag for later use, allowing you to take out only the number of rolls needed for a given meal. People with smaller households may also find it useful to freeze dough for later baking. Since most recipes make two large loaves, if you will only use one before the other would be old or risking mold, freeze the second loaf to use the next time. Freezing the dough itself is preferable to freezing the baked bread (although certainly this is an option, too), because the end product will better retain its freshness and texture.

If you do decide to make your dough ahead of time and freeze it, the best way to do this is to place the shaped loaves (or disks) on a wax paper-lined cookie sheet, freeze (uncovered) and then place in a tight plastic bag once frozen solid.

This gives you much information to think about and a number of options and ideas, but now it's time to move on to what we are all really here for – the bread! You are now well-informed, well-armed, and well-educated with all the basics you need to know, and it's time to get baking!

Everyday Stand-By White Bread

Everyone needs at least one go-to bread recipe, especially if you intend to make all (or most) of your breads at home on a regular basis. This white bread recipe is a reliable bread that can be used every day and performs very, very well whether as a dinnertime side, a sandwich bread, or a basic dough for almost anything from dinner rolls to pizza dough. If I could only have one recipe in my arsenal, this would be it.

· 6 ½ cups all-purpose flour
· 3 tablespoons sugar
· 1 tablespoon salt
· 3 tablespoons lard (or butter or shortening)
· 1 ½ tablespoons instant yeast
· 2 ½ cups very warm water (about 120°)

Place all dry ingredients and the lard in the mixer bowl, including the yeast. Using the flat beater attachment, mix dry ingredients and lard through for 1 to 2 minutes on the "stir" or lowest setting. Mix just until mixture looks uniform.

With the mixer still running, pour in the warm water. Continue to mix just until the dough forms and begins to come together as a ball (30 seconds to a minute).

Stop the mixer, remove the flat beater and place the dough hook onto your stand mixer. Set on first (stir) or second speed and let the mixer knead the dough for 6 to 8 minutes.

After kneading turn off the mixer and remove the dough hook. Let the dough rest in the bowl for 10 minutes.

Meanwhile, grease 2 loaf pans. After the dough has rested for 10 minutes, form the dough into 2 loaves and place in pans, turning once to coat top with grease and help prevent sticking to the cover. Cover with a clean, damp towel or oiled plastic wrap and let rise in a warm place until doubled (about an inch above the rim of the loaf pan).

Bake at 350° for 20-25 minutes, until nicely browned.

Additional Uses for Everyday White Bread

As mentioned with the Everyday White Bread Recipe, this bread dough can be used for almost anything you can imagine to deliver a different, but still excellent, product. This easily-prepared, easily-memorized bread dough can be used to make any of the following (and probably more not yet thought of!). Simply prepare the dough as in the recipe, then shape and bake accordingly as noted:

Pizza Crust: Divide prepared dough into three equal parts (two for a thicker or larger pizza, more for smaller or personal-size pizzas). Press each part out on a large baking sheet. Bake for about 10 minutes in a 375° oven. Remove, top as desired, and return to oven, baking until cheese melts and pizza is done (about 15-20 minutes).

Dinner Rolls: Prepare dough and divide into 24 even pieces, about 2 inches round, rolling into balls (smaller or larger as desired is okay, too). Grease two 9x13 pans. Place rolled dough into pans, almost touching but with room to rise. Cover and rise until doubled (about 20 to 30 minutes). Bake in a 350° oven for 15 to 20 minutes.

Cheesy Garlic Bread Sticks: Prepare dough as directed. Grease two large cookie sheets. Divide dough into two equal balls and pat each ball out to fill each pan. With a flat-bladed knife or a pastry cutter, cut down the center of the dough lengthwise, then cut at intervals about one inch across in the opposite direction. Sprinkle all over with garlic powder, then shredded cheese (mozzarella or cheddar are good choices). Bake in a 375° oven for 15-18 minutes.

Garlic Knots: Prepare dough as directed. Divide into about 24 balls. On a lightly floured surface, roll each ball into a short, fat rope. Form into a loose knot. Place on greased baking sheets and bake at 350° about 15 minutes or until done. Meanwhile, melt one cup butter with three or four cloves minced garlic and set aside. When knots are baked through, remove from oven and let cool a few minutes, then dip entire knot in the melted butter mixture and place on pan to set. Best enjoyed warm.

Sandwich and Burger Rolls: Prepare dough as directed. Divide into 12 to 14 even (more or less, depending on how large you want your rolls to be), large balls and place on greased cookie sheet, leaving room to rise without touching. Let rise until doubled. Bake in 350° for 20 to 25 minutes. For a softer top, brush tops with melted butter while still hot. Cool on wire rack, cut in half and serve. For a crustier roll, leave untouched or brush with a beaten egg white prior to baking.

Cinnamon Swirl Bread (with or without raisins): (Makes two loaves) Prepare as for white bread. Divide into two balls. Roll or pat out each ball separately on a lightly-floured surface to about 8 inches wide by 14 inches long. Sprinkle entire surface with cinnamon sugar. Sprinkle with raisins if desired. Roll into a loaf, starting with the short side. Pinch bottom seam to seal. Place in greased bread pan, cover and rise until double. Bake at 350° 20 to 25 minutes. *Note: When making Everyday White Bread, simply use one half of the dough to make a cinnamon-swirl loaf and one half for regular white bread for both sandwich bread and a tasty morning treat with one batch!*

Cinnamon Buns: Prepare dough as directed but increase sugar to four tablespoons and increase the instant yeast to two full tablespoons. Using butter as the fat instead of lard makes a tastier roll. Divide into two equal balls. Roll or pat each ball separately on a lightly floured surface to flatten, to about 11x15. Spread entire surface with very soft butter. Sprinkle generously with ground cinnamon. Roll, starting with the long side, and place the seam on the bottom. Cut into 1 inch rolls and place on greased baking sheets. Bake at 350° for about 20 minutes. Glaze with a mixture of confectioner's sugar and milk while still warm. Best if served warm.

Bread Bowls: Prepare dough as normal. Divide into six even balls. Grease two baking sheets, shape balls into rounds, and place with plenty of room to rise without touching (so that crust forms without any soft spots). Let rise until about doubled in size. Bake in 350° oven for 20 minutes. Let brown more than usual for a firmer crust. Let cool for several hours before using, or even overnight (in a cold oven uncovered is a good way to preserve the firm crust). When ready to use, cut flat across the top about 1/3 of the way down, low enough down to make a good-sized opening. Pull out the soft interior and serve with soup, chili, etc.

Amish White Bread

This Amish White Bread is another white bread option, and one that returns regularly reliable results. It's an excellent bread for a beginner and also one that has a very good structure for sandwiches and daily eating. It is very similar to the Everyday White Bread but is quite a bit sweeter, which may or may not be to your liking. It also tends to be a fast and easy riser (often needing just a half an hour) so if your home tends to challenge you when it comes time to rise your breads, give this recipe a try.

- 6 cups all-purpose flour
- 2/3 cup sugar
- 1 ½ teaspoons salt
- 1 ½ tablespoons instant yeast
- ¼ cup oil
- 2 cups very warm water (about 120°)

Place all dry ingredients and the oil in the mixer bowl, including the yeast. Using the flat beater attachment, mix dry ingredients and oil through for 1 to 2 minutes on the "stir" or lowest setting, just until mixture looks uniform.

With the mixer still running, pour in the warm water. Continue to mix just until the dough forms and begins to come together as a ball (30 seconds to a minute).

Stop the mixer, remove the flat beater and place the dough hook onto your stand mixer. Set on first (stir) or second speed and let the mixer knead the dough for 6 to 8 minutes.

After kneading, turn off the mixer and remove the dough hook. Let the dough rest in the bowl for 10 minutes.

Meanwhile, grease 2 loaf pans. After the dough has rested for 10 minutes, form the dough into 2 loaves and place in pans, turning once to coat top with grease and help prevent sticking to the cover. Cover with a clean, damp towel or oiled plastic wrap and let rise in a warm place until doubled (about an inch above the rim of the loaf pan).

Bake at 350° for 30 minutes, until nicely browned.

Honey Wheat Bread

Wheat breads are not only a nice change from the white bread routine but they are also healthier, being a source of whole grains. While this particular wheat bread recipe does include white flour, it is more than 50% whole wheat flour which will help you cut down on the amount of refined flours in your diet and help you to reach your daily quota of whole grains. Cutting the wheat flour half and half with white flour results in a softer bread that does not overpower, preventing the bitter flavor some people are sensitive to in 100% wheat breads yet it still maintains a flexible crumb for sandwiches and more. Many people find this a more palatable option over 100% wheat bread, especially for children, making it a good middle ground. The use of honey instead of white sugar nicely complements the wheat flavor while further reducing refined ingredients in the diet and resulting in a flavorful bread that you'll feel good about serving.

This honey wheat dough, like the Everyday White Bread, is also a good, versatile recipe to use for Honey Wheat dinner rolls.

- 3 cups all-purpose flour
- 3 ½ cups whole wheat flour
- 3 tablespoons honey
- 1 tablespoon salt
- 3 tablespoons butter (or lard)
- 1 ½ tablespoons instant yeast
- 2 ½ cups very warm water (about 120°)

Place the two flours, salt, butter or lard, and yeast in the mixer bowl. Using the flat beater attachment, mix the dry ingredients and butter through for 1 to 2 minutes on the "stir" or lowest setting. Mix just until the mixture looks uniform and the butter looks to be distributed fairly evenly throughout.

Measure the very warm water into a measuring cup and then add the honey to the water. With the mixer still running, pour the warm water and honey into the dry ingredients. Continue to mix just until the dough forms and begins to come together as a ball (30 seconds to a minute).

Stop the mixer, remove the flat beater, and place the dough hook onto your stand mixer. Set on first (stir) or second speed and let the mixer knead the dough for 6 to 8 minutes. You want the dough to be of moderate firmness; not hard but not sticky to the touch (a bit tacky is okay at this stage). You may add an additional ½ cup of white flour if needed to reach desired consistency.

After kneading, turn the mixer off and remove the dough hook. Let the dough rest in the bowl for 10 minutes.

Meanwhile, grease 2 loaf pans. After the dough has rested for 10 minutes, form the dough into 2 loaves and place them in the greased pans. Turn once to coat with grease (helps to keep the dough moist when rising and to help prevent the cover from sticking). Cover with a clean, damp towel or oiled/sprayed plastic wrap and let rise in a warm place until doubled (about an inch above the rim of the loaf pan).

Bake at 350° for 20-25 minutes, until nicely browned. Lightly brush top with butter while warm if desired (this adds flavor and also helps to keep a softer outer crust).

Rye Bread

Rye bread is a very popular choice, ranking high after white bread. Like the Honey Wheat Bread, this recipe incorporates whole grain rye with white flour to achieve a nice, moderate density while really letting the rye flavor come through. Sweetening with brown sugar instead of white helps "darken" the flavor as well. It's a fast and easy way to make rye bread at home, get in some good grains, and enjoy this favorite. You're sure to find this recipe just as easy to prepare with this stand mixer bread method, and rye lovers will appreciate having this recipe in the box.

· **4 cups all-purpose flour**
· **2 cups Rye flour**
· **¼ cup brown sugar**
· **2 tablespoons caraway seeds**
· **1 tablespoon salt**
· **1 tablespoon instant yeast**
· **¼ cup oil**
· **2 cups very warm water (about 120°)**

Place all dry ingredients and the oil (can substitute melted butter or fat, lard, etc.) in the mixer bowl, including the yeast. Using the flat beater attachment, mix the dry ingredients and oil through for 1 to 2 minutes on the "stir" or lowest setting. Mix just until mixture looks uniform.

With the mixer still running, pour in the warm water. Continue to mix just until the dough forms and begins to come together as a ball (30 seconds to a minute).

Stop the mixer, remove the flat beater and place the dough hook onto your stand mixer. Set on first (stir) or second speed and let the mixer knead the dough for 6 to 8 minutes. Add an additional ½ cup white flour if needed as the dough kneads to build proper consistency (moderately firm, not too sticky).

After kneading, turn off the mixer and remove the dough hook. Let the dough rest in the bowl for 10 minutes.

Meanwhile, prepare pans. This bread may be baked in regular loaf pans (will make two loaves), or may be baked on a greased or parchment-paper lined baking sheet, formed into two round balls and spaced for rising (like a traditional round rye loaf). Slash the tops of the loaves prior to rising. Cover loaves with a clean, damp towel or oiled plastic wrap and let rise in a warm place until doubled.

Bake at 350° for 25 minutes, until nicely browned.

Golden Egg Bread

This egg bread is a nice way to incorporate more protein into your diet along with your daily grains. It is more dense than a typical plain white bread, but the flavor is very close (with, of course, a mild egg taste). The denser crumb stands up well for toast and sandwiches without being in competition with spreads or fillers. It is an excellent choice for kid's lunchboxes for age-old favorites like peanut butter and jelly, but won't disappoint more "mature" palates, either. Although excellent warm and fresh from the oven, as a sandwich bread it often benefits from standing (wrapped or stored) overnight or for a day before cutting, which helps the crumb to hold its shape. This also means that it maintains its freshness well for a few days, and so you don't have to worry if you don't use it up right away. Golden Egg Bread is a moister bread, contributing to its ability to hang around and still present an excellent texture and flavor.

- 6 ½ cups all-purpose flour
- 4 tablespoons sugar
- 1 tablespoon salt
- 1 tablespoon plus 1 teaspoon instant yeast
- 4 tablespoons lard
- 2 eggs
- 2 cups very warm water (about 120°)

Place all dry ingredients (including yeast) and the lard in the mixer bowl. Using the flat beater attachment, mix the dry ingredients and lard through for 1 to 2 minutes on the "stir" or lowest setting. Mix just until mixture looks uniform and fat is incorporated throughout.

With the mixer still running, pour in the warm water. Continue to mix just until the dough forms and begins to come together as a ball (30 seconds to a minute).

Stop the mixer, remove the flat beater and place the dough hook onto your stand mixer. Set on first (stir) or second speed and let the mixer knead the dough for 6 to 8 minutes. Add up to an additional ½ cup white flour if needed as the dough kneads to build proper consistency (moderately firm, not too sticky but not too soft).

After kneading, turn off the mixer and remove the dough hook. Let the dough rest in the bowl for 10 minutes.

Meanwhile, grease two bread pans. After resting, shape dough into two loaves and place in pans. Cover loaves with a clean, damp towel or oiled plastic wrap and let rise in a warm place until doubled.

Bake at 350° for 20-25 minutes, until done.

Old Fashioned Potato Bread

Potato bread is popular with many people. A firmer bread with good moisture and its own subtly unique flavor, it makes an excellent sandwich bread (or even a great roll!). This recipe is also a great way to use up any leftover cooked potatoes, including boiled, baked, or mashed; just be sure to remove any remaining skins, mash well with a fork, and use in equal amounts as called for in this recipe. If using leftover mashed potatoes, unless the potatoes are heavily seasoned or flavored (such as with garlic), normal seasonings like salt and pepper tend to disappear in the bread, so not to worry.

If you do cook the potato expressly for the purpose of preparing this recipe, you'll want to cook two medium to large potatoes to get a cup of mashed (obviously depending on the size of the potato!). Reserve the cooking liquid, let cool to 120° F, and use in place of the water in the recipe (if you do not have a full two cups of liquid left after boiling, simply use what you have and make up the rest with very warm water). This will give you an even more robust potato flavor that you'll really enjoy.

· 6 ½ cups all-purpose flour plus one tablespoon to dust loaves before baking
· 3 tablespoons sugar
· 1 tablespoon salt
· 1 ½ tablespoons instant yeast
· 2 tablespoons butter
· 1 cup cooked potato, mashed
· 2 cups very warm water (about 120°) or reserved potato water

Cook potato and mash well with a fork or potato masher. Set aside.

Place flour, sugar, salt, yeast, and butter in the mixer bowl. Mix through with the flat beater attachment for about 30 seconds on the "stir" or lowest setting. Add the potatoes and mix for about one more minute to distribute throughout. Next, with the mixer running, add the warm water and continue to mix just until the dough forms and begins to come together as a ball (30 seconds to a minute).

Stop the mixer; remove the flat beater and place the dough hook onto your stand mixer. Set on first (stir) or second speed and let the mixer knead the dough for 6 to 8 minutes until you have a moderately firm dough.

After kneading, turn off the mixer and remove the dough hook. Let the dough rest in the bowl for 10 minutes.

Meanwhile, grease two bread pans. Divide dough in half and shape into loaves, then place in prepared pans. Cover loaves with a clean, damp towel or oiled plastic wrap and let rise in a warm place until doubled.

Just before baking, lightly brush tops of the loaves with water and dust lightly with additional flour.

Bake at 375° for 40-45 minutes, until done.

Rustic Honey Oatmeal Bread

Oatmeal is yet another great way to increase whole grains in the diet and it tends to be one that is more kid-friendly, too. As a matter of fact, my kids actually ASK me to make this bread for them! It has a touch of sweetness to it and is another of the firmer breads. This Rustic Oatmeal bread is just a bit of a darker bread, too, but is still light enough for white bread purists. The slightly sweet flavor makes it an excellent choice for egg salads, toast and jam, or with a nicely salted butter. Incidentally, if you are looking for a darker oatmeal bread (for instance, one that will pair well with things like barbeque, ham, and baked beans), try replacing the honey in this recipe with molasses instead – perfect!

· **6 ½ cups all-purpose flour**
· **1 cup quick oats**
· **2 teaspoons salt**
· **1 ½ tablespoons instant yeast**
· **½ cup melted butter**
· **½ cup honey**
· **2 eggs**
· **1 ½ cups very warm water (about 120°)**

To top:
· **1 tablespoon water**
· **1 egg white**
· **Oats (either rolled or quick oats)**

Place the flour, quick oats, salt, and instant yeast together in the bowl of your stand mixer. With the flat beater attachment, mix on "Stir" (or first) setting just to lightly mix the dry ingredients through. Add the melted butter, honey, warm water (mix together water and honey if you prefer), and the eggs. Mix again on low setting just until ingredients mix through and combine into a ball on the flat beater.

Stop the mixer, remove the flat beater and place the dough hook onto your stand mixer. Set on first (stir) or second speed and let the mixer knead the dough for 6 to 8 minutes. Add up to an additional ½ cup white flour if needed as the dough kneads to build proper consistency (moderately firm and elastic).

After kneading, turn off the mixer and remove the dough hook. Let the dough rest in the bowl for 10 minutes.

Meanwhile, grease two bread pans. After resting shape the dough into two loaves and place in pans.

Mix together the tablespoon of water and egg white. Beat lightly with a fork. Brush over tops of loaves and then sprinkle loaves with additional oats.

Cover loaves with a clean, damp towel or oiled plastic wrap and let rise in a warm place until doubled.

Bake at 375° for 40 minutes, until done.

100% Whole Wheat Bread

*Here is a wheat bread recipe that honestly is 100% whole grain wheat. Naturally that means you can't expect it to be as soft and high-rising as a white flour bread, but this recipe delivers a firm bread with good moisture and flavor that is a good all-around whole grain bread for sandwiches, meal sides, toast and more. Do note – because bulk is lost in the decreased rising and action of the whole wheat flour, this recipe prepares just **one loaf**.*

· **5 cups whole wheat flour**
· **1/3 cup brown sugar**
· **2 teaspoons salt**
· **1 ½ tablespoons instant yeast**
· **1/3 cup oil**
· **2 cups very warm milk (about 120°)**

Place the wheat flour, salt, and instant yeast together in the bowl of your stand mixer. With the flat beater attachment, mix on "Stir" (or first) setting just to lightly mix the dry ingredients through. Add the oil and mix through for a few turns. With the mixer running on low, pour in the warmed milk. Continue to mix on low setting just until ingredients mix through and combine into a ball on the flat beater. (Note the consistency of this dough will be a bit different; stay on the side of soft and a bit wetter with this recipe to maintain good end moisture and consistency).

Stop the mixer, remove the flat beater and place the dough hook onto your stand mixer. Set on first (stir) or second speed and let the mixer knead the dough for 6 minutes, until the dough comes together as a ball. If the dough is not forming a ball on the hook, add up to one additional cup of wheat flour but no more than ¼ cup at a time.

After kneading, turn off the mixer and remove the dough hook. Let the dough rest in the bowl for 15 minutes. (You can actually let this rest as long as 20 minutes, which gives the whole wheat more time to absorb moisture.)

Meanwhile, grease a bread pan. After resting shape the dough into a loaf and place in the pan. If you like you may also form this into a round or oval loaf and bake on a baking sheet. Cover the loaf with a clean, damp towel or oiled plastic wrap and let rise in a warm place until about 1 ½ times its size.

Bake at 375° for 40 minutes, until done. For a softer crust, brush the hot loaf with butter immediately after baking.

Six-Grain Multigrain Bread

Multigrain breads offer us both dietary and gustatory benefits. Whether you are looking for something to boost your grain intake or for a bread with a more complex flavor, this multigrain bread is sure to please. Multigrain breads, like completely whole wheat products, can often be more time-consuming and involved, but this simplified method is easy enough for you to make every day.

- 3 cups all-purpose flour
- 1 cup whole wheat flour
- ½ cup bran
- 1 cup rolled oats
- ½ cup cornmeal
- ½ cup unsalted sunflower seeds (or sesame seeds)
- ½ cup flax seed
- 2 teaspoons salt
- 1 ½ tablespoons instant yeast
- ¼ cup melted butter
- ¼ cup honey
- 2 eggs
- 2 cups water

Place white flour, wheat flour, bran, oats, cornmeal, sunflower seeds, flax, salt, and yeast in the mixer bowl. Using the flat beater attachment, mix dry ingredients through for 30 seconds to 1 minute.

Add the melted butter, honey, and eggs and turn the mixer on to "stir" (or low). With the mixer running, add the water and continue to mix just until the dough forms and begins to come together as a ball (30 seconds to a minute).

Stop the mixer, remove the flat beater and place the dough hook onto your stand mixer. Set on first (stir) or second speed and let the mixer knead the dough for 6 to 8 minutes.

After kneading, turn off the mixer and remove the dough hook. Let the dough rest in the bowl for 15 minutes.

Meanwhile, grease 2 loaf pans. After the dough has rested form the dough into 2 loaves and place in greased pans, turning once to coat (alternatively, because this bread does not rise as high as white bread, you might prefer to make one large, round or oval loaf on a baking sheet). Cover with a clean, damp towel or oiled plastic wrap and let rise in a warm place until a little less than doubled.

(Optional) Just before baking, if desired, combine one egg white with one tablespoon of water, brush over the top of the loaves and then sprinkle with some additional oats and/or sunflower seeds.

Bake at 350° for 35 to 40 minutes, until done.

Fantastic Fast French Bread

Not only is this an outstanding bread to serve with all sorts of meals (soups and pastas in particular!), but it is very fast to prepare. It uses the same basic quick method but rises very quickly as well, so it is particularly good when you want a nice bread for a side in just a little time. What's even better is that everyone loves this bread. A real fan-favorite!

· **6 ½ cups all-purpose flour**
· **2 tablespoons sugar**
· **2 tablespoons oil**
· **2 teaspoons salt**
· **1 ½ tablespoons instant yeast**
· **2 ½ cups very warm water**

· **Cornmeal (for baking pan)**
· **1 egg white (for top)**
· **1 tablespoon water (for top)**

Place the flour, sugar, salt, oil, and yeast in the mixer bowl. Using the flat paddle, run the mixer to combine ingredients on "stir" or lowest setting. While running, add the warm water and continue to stir just until combined and the dough begins to form a ball.

Stop the mixer, remove the flat paddle and attach the dough hook. Set the mixer to the first (stir) or second setting and knead for 6 to 8 minutes. After kneading, stop, remove dough hook, and let the dough rest for 10 minutes.

Meanwhile, prepare the baking pan(s). Grease a baking sheet and sprinkle it with the cornmeal. (An 11x17 inch cookie sheet is ideal and will usually fit both loaves on one sheet, each to a side, but you may prefer to place just one per sheet so they don't rise into each other. If using anything smaller than an 11x17, place only one loaf per sheet and if the pan is shorter than 15 inches, place diagonally for more length.)

After the dough rests for 10 minutes, divide the dough into two equal balls. To shape, you may either shape the dough into a long (about 15 inch) cylinder shape or pat the dough out on a floured surface (stretching to about 10x15) and then roll the dough (starting with the long side) to form a 15-inch long roll. Seal the end seams and place on prepared baking sheet, seam down. Cover with a damp towel or oiled plastic wrap and let rise until nearly doubled, about 30 to 45 minutes. (Note: you may also divide this dough into several pieces and shape it into small, individual-size loaves.)

Just before baking, whisk the egg white and add the tablespoon of water, whisking to combine. Brush over the tops of the loaves. If desired, sprinkle the top of the loaves with sesame seeds for Sesame French Bread.

Bake at 400° for 20-25 minutes, until nicely browned.

Rustic Italian Bread

Nothing goes better with a thick tomato sauce than a thick chunk of crusty Italian bread. Of course, this recipe is more versatile at pairing than that and it makes excellent garlic bread, too. It's an ideal recipe to have in your box of old reliables. What's doubly nice is that this easy stand mixer bread recipe makes two large loaves so you can share, freeze one for later, or just have more to enjoy!

· **6 cups all-purpose flour**
· **4 teaspoons sugar**
· **1 ½ teaspoons salt**
· **1 ½ tablespoons instant yeast**
· **¼ cup olive oil**
· **2 ½ cups very warm milk**

· **Cornmeal (for baking pan)**
· **2 egg whites (for top)**

Warm the milk to around 120° (can be done either on the stovetop or in the microwave). Set aside but keep hot.

Place all the dry ingredients and the yeast in the bowl of your mixer. With the paddle attachment on, mix through to distribute dry ingredients evenly.

With the mixer still running, pour in the warm milk and oil. Continue to mix just until the dough forms and begins to come together as a ball (30 seconds to a minute).

Stop the mixer, remove the flat beater and place the dough hook onto your stand mixer. Set on first (stir) or second speed and let the mixer knead the dough for 6 to 8 minutes.

After kneading, turn off the mixer and remove the dough hook. Let the dough rest in the bowl for 10 minutes.

Sprinkle two baking sheets with cornmeal or corn flour. Divide dough into two even balls and shape each into a round or oval shape. Place on pans and slash tops diagonally using a sharp, flat-bladed knife. Cover with a clean, damp towel or oiled plastic wrap and let rise in a warm place until doubled.

After rising, beat the egg white with a fork and lightly brush all over the loaves.

Bake at 375° for 25-35 minutes.

*Note: To make garlic bread, prepare Italian bread as above, then let cool for 20-30 minutes (to make it easier to cut without crushing; alternatively, store the bread until ready to use and then prepare). Melt ¼ cup butter per loaf and add one or two minced garlic cloves. Sprinkle in some parsley if desired as well.

Cut the prepared loaf in half lengthwise. Brush the exposed interior halves with the garlic and butter mixture. Bake at 375° for 10 minutes, until butter starts to brown slightly and bread is heated through. You may also heat under a broiler (about 5 minutes) but do keep a close eye as the bread can over-brown quickly.

Dinner Rolls

While it's true that the Everyday White Bread recipe makes an excellent dinner roll dough as well, this dinner roll recipe offers just a little more of a robust flavor. The addition of egg and butter round out the flavors for a delicious, hearty roll to accompany any meal.

· 5 cups all-purpose flour
· 3 tablespoons sugar
· ½ teaspoon salt
· 4 teaspoons instant yeast
· ¼ cup melted butter
· 1 egg
· 1 ½ cups warm water

Place the flour, sugar, salt, yeast, and melted butter together in the mixer bowl and mix to combine until evenly distributed (about 30 seconds to one minute). Add the egg and mix to combine.

With the mixer still running, pour in the warm water. Continue to mix just until the dough forms and begins to come together as a ball (30 seconds to a minute).

Stop the mixer, remove the flat beater and attach the dough hook to your stand mixer. Set on first (stir) or second speed and let the mixer knead the dough for 6 to 8 minutes.

After kneading, turn off the mixer and remove the dough hook. Let the dough rest in the bowl for 10 minutes.

Meanwhile, grease two 9x13 pans. After the dough has rested for 10 minutes, form the dough into 1 ½ inch balls and place in pans (should make about 24, fewer if balls are larger). Cover with a clean, damp towel or oiled plastic wrap and let rise in a warm place until doubled.

Bake at 350° for 20 minutes, until nicely browned. If desired, brush tops with melted butter while hot.

Crescent Rolls

If you're looking for something a little different yet impressive to pair with your meals, be sure to try this easy Crescent Roll recipe. Buttery and light, they really make you shine; everyone at your table will think you spent hours perfecting these delicious horns. Incidentally, this homemade recipe is a great substitution in recipes calling for refrigerator-aisle crescent rolls, opening a world of possibilities to you without the cost and extraneous ingredients and preservatives.

· **4 ½ to 5 cups all-purpose flour**
· **2 teaspoons salt**
· **¼ cup sugar**
· **2 tablespoons instant yeast**
· **½ cup butter, cut into chunks**
· **1 egg**
· **⅔ cup very warm milk**
· **1 ⅓ cups very warm water**

Place two cups of the flour in the stand mixer bowl, then add the salt, sugar, and yeast. Run for several seconds (with paddle attachment) on stir (low) just to mix the dry ingredients evenly. Add butter chunks and run until the mixer cuts the butter throughout (if necessary, to avoid butter chunking, increase speed for this step).

Heat milk in microwave or on stove top to about 120° (if not using a thermometer, very warm to the touch, but not hot enough to burn). Next add the egg and warm milk and water to the dry ingredients. Mix on stir/low speed until wet.

With the mixer running, begin adding the remaining flour to the wet mix ½ cup at a time. Do not use more than 5 cups total flour. (This will be a very soft, light dough, slightly sticky, and less firm than the other bread doughs).

After all the flour has been added, replace the flat paddle with the dough hook and knead for 6 minutes on the lowest setting. After dough is kneaded, stop the mixer, remove the dough hook and let the dough rest in the bowl for 15 minutes (a little longer rest period helps to firm this dough slightly, absorb moisture, and make it more workable in the next step).

After resting, turn dough out onto a floured surface and divide in half, forming each into a ball. Set aside one half and roll the first ball out into a circle to between ¼ and ½ inch thick. Now, cut the dough into 16 evenly triangles (start by halving the circle, then quartering, and so on). Note: you may cut these rolls into fewer slices if you prefer larger crescent rolls. There's really no limit to size, just be aware that you may need to adjust the baking time slightly.

Starting with the wide end, roll the wedges to the point and tuck the point underneath the roll. Place rolls on a greased or (preferably) parchment-lined baking sheet, leaving space for rising.

Let rise until doubled (usually ½ to 1 hour).

Bake at 375° for 15 to 20 minutes, until golden brown. Brush with melted butter while hot.

Just Like Homemade, Only Better

If you are familiar with traditional methods of bread making, you can probably already tell how much easier and *faster* these recipes will be without even having tried one. This basic method and these basic recipes give you an excellent set of options for freshly-made breads for every day and for any occasion.

Nothing can beat the taste, smell, or healthfulness of bread you bake fresh at home without extraneous conditioners, preservatives, and other unnecessary agents. The purpose of this book and of other of my titles are to help people get back to eating well, taking and putting pride in their food, and finding ways to do that in a world that has left us with little time and energy to spare for this all-important task of feeding ourselves well. It's real eating made possible for real life in the new millennium.

Hopefully these recipes and the information in this book have given you the confidence you need to be able to put high-quality, great-tasting breads on your table on a regular basis. Thank you for reading and I hope you have become inspired to feed yourself and all of yours well. And now...

...It's time to bake bread!

Enjoy!

About the Author

Homesteading, house-holding, farming, gardening, being a wife and mother, and yes writing, too, represent the majority of ways Mary Ellen Ward spends her days. Believing in living well and eating well and days that end in a feeling of accomplishment, these things that seem a lot like "work" to others are the things she truly enjoys, and the ways she chooses to spend her days. She considers herself highly fortunate to be able to do so, and enjoys sharing her knowledge and experiences with others with similar inclinations.

Look for more titles to come, including additional "Daily Bread" titles, from Mary in the near future.

Other Books by Mary Ellen Ward

Other books by Mary Ellen Ward you may also enjoy include:

Make Ahead Mix Day: Complete Instructions for On-Hand Homemade Quick Mixes
(available now on Kindle, compatible apps and eReaders, and also in paperback)

A Drink for All Seasons: Winter and the Holidays
(available now on Kindle, compatible apps and eReaders, and also in paperback)

Please look for more titles to come by Mary Ellen Ward on Amazon.com and visit her author page (on Amazon, click on the live-linked author name) where you can find a list of all current, new, and upcoming releases by Mary. Be a part of Mary's community of followers and check out pictures she shares, blog posts and important links, along with her biography and more.

The Homemade Homestead

You can also find Mary Ellen Ward sharing her life, tips, tricks, current projects and other books and resources at her website, TheHomemadeHomestead.com. To be easily updated with new posts, please subscribe to **The Homemade Homestead** through the link available on-site.

You may also like to email Mary Ward to be added to her contact list. The list will be used *only* to update subscribers of important news, such as new books and interesting happenings. Please rest assured that your contact will be used *only* for updates from this author and her website, and will *never* be sold to a third party without your permission! To be added to the list, please use the *Contact* Page at The Homemade Homestead.

~If you have enjoyed this book and/or found any small part of it useful, your honest review will be very much appreciated by both the author and fellow and future readers. Thoughtful reviews help good books to be found!~

Thank You

Notes

Made in the USA
Coppell, TX
07 November 2021